THE
CONTROLLING
ABSENTEEISM POCKETBOOK

C000040568

By Max A. Eggert
Drawings by Phil Hailstone

"Excellent – full of really good tips, some which act as a reminder, others totally new which we are planning to put into practice."
Deborah Moss, Company Secretary, Wirefield Ltd

Published by:
Management Pocketbooks Ltd
Laurel House, Station Approach, Alresford, Hants SO24 9JH, U.K.
Tel: +44 (0)1962 735573   Fax: +44 (0)1962 733637
E-mail: sales@pocketbook.co.uk
Website: www.pocketbook.co.uk

This edition published 2000.   Reprinted 2004.

© Max A. Eggert 2000

British Library Cataloguing-in-Publication Data – A catalogue record for this book is available
from the British Library.

ISBN 1 870471 64 4

Design, typesetting and graphics by **efex ltd**.   Printed in U.K.

CONTENTS

AUTHOR'S INTRODUCTION

As I write this book not 400 metres from Bondi Beach in Sydney, Australia, with the summer sun encouraging the temperature into the high twenties, and this morning's surf report suggesting that the sea is warming up nicely, I know where I would rather be and it is not at my computer.

The choice is what the Americans call a 'no brainer'. If I was working in a boring, repetitive job with unfriendly people, in an unsafe environment, for a management that had long lunch breaks and played golf regularly with clients, I would definitely be out of here. If my children were ill or there was some domestic crisis the choice again would be easy. If I had enough money to get by for even a few weeks, I would much rather be doing things for myself than for someone else. When I think about these things I am amazed that absence is as low as it is.

This Pocketbook examines why people take time off, and what a caring, committed and professional management can reasonably do about it. If you are one of those managers who think most people are lazy, deviant and, given the chance, will fiddle the system to get time off then this is definitely not the book for you.

What is attempted here is to provide some suggestions for management, and perhaps trade unions, to help employees fulfil their employment contracts and support them in time of need when they are unable to make work because of sickness or some significant domestic strain. Any employer who thinks that his or her employees are machines or automatons, and should never take a day off work, to my mind falls sadly short on the ethical responsibilities of management. This book is written in the hope that there will be mutual respect, fairness and understanding on both sides of the management divide.

Be successful.

Max A. Eggert
Bondi Beach

DEDICATION

To Pony, Val, Pam, Sheila, Joyce, Kathy
and all the line supervisors at
Knowles Electronics who made
my attendance figures look good.

1NTRODUCTION

INTRODUCTION

TOWARDS A DEFINITION

If you are going to attempt to control absence it is important to understand what it is, so we start with some definitions.

Absence is an employee's non-availability for work when work is available for that employee.

This is a good start but is not specific enough. It would also embrace things like holidays, time off for safety meetings or doctor's appointments (which are usually official absences in that they are approved by management). So we can look at absence in three different ways:

Statutory or Legal absence: Maternity leave, safety rep training, public duties, etc
Authorised absence: Holidays, sickness, and compassionate leave
Casual absence: Unauthorised absence and *lead swinging*

Usually it is casual absence that managements wish to reduce to a minimum. They also sometimes have problems with employees whose sickness is such that it is detrimental to production or the services the organisation provides.

COSTS OF ABSENTEEISM

- **Wages** - Overtime costs, pay for extra workers or contractors to cover the work of those absent
- **Redeployment** - Moving staff away from their regular work to more urgent work for which they might not be trained
- **Benefits** - Paying sick pay to those who are not as sick as they claim to be
- **Administration** - Money spent on the collection of absence data, administration of sick pay schemes, plus the cost of the sick pay itself and the cost of hiring and training surplus labour
- **Production or service losses** - Lower productivity, lower quality, plus costs of production and/or delivery delays and customer disenchantment
- **Overhead** - Plant and equipment standing idle owing to absenteeism; increase in overhead cost ratios when production or service falls

The first four are more easily determined than the last two, which are perhaps indirect rather than direct costs, but can be significant.

PSYCHOLOGICAL COSTS

Here are some additional psychological costs, which are more difficult to quantify but nevertheless very real.

- Increased pressure on those who have to cover for absent workmates
- Higher accident rates due to stress of extra work or through doing work for which employees have not been trained
- Increased pressure on supervisors who have to manage with fewer people or people not as skilled
- Frustration in terms of planning when unexpected absence causes rescheduling
- Interpersonal friction at work between those with good attendance and those who *swing the lead*, and the damage this does to teamworking
- Management time in disciplining those who are found to be taking unauthorised absence
- Poor morale due to the perceived unfairness of the system which allows abuse

THE MEASUREMENT OF ABSENCE

Measurement is one of the major keys to the control of absence. Without measurement you can have no idea how bad or acceptable your situation is, how you compare to other organisations similar to yours, or whether or not the control strategies you put in place are working.

You need measurement to be able to make comparisons between individuals, departments, plants, locations and overtime. You need measurement to identify patterns of absence on different days or seasons, or absence relating to other variables such as strike activity or accidents.

Because so many variables bring about casual absence, you need to be reasonably sophisticated in the way you measure. For example, straight 'lost time' will not distinguish between a few people taking extended time off and lots of people casually taking single days off.

FIVE WAYS OF MEASURING ABSENCE

Lost time rate

$$\frac{\text{Number of working days or hours lost}}{\text{Total number of possible working days or hours}} \times 100$$

Days lost per employee

$$\frac{\text{Number of working days lost in a year or month}}{\text{Average number of employees per year or month}}$$

Average length of absence

$$\frac{\text{Total number of days lost}}{\text{Total number of absences}}$$

Individual frequency

$$\frac{\text{Number of employees absent one or more times}}{\text{Average number of employees}} \times 100$$

Frequency rate

$$\frac{\text{Number of individual absences per year or month}}{\text{Average numbers employed per year or month}} \times 100$$

You have to decide whether the cost of getting this information is worth the value. Sometimes the cost of obtaining information is more expensive than the absenteeism it might prevent. Even for small companies a computerised system easily pays for itself as attendance improves.

SOME PROBLEMS WITH MEASUREMENT

Even when you measure absenteeism there are some limitations, of which the sensible manager should be aware. They include:

- **Difficulties with definition**
  The way you define absenteeism will limit the number of comparisons that you can make.

- **Difficulties with data collection**
  True classification is difficult and not uniform. For example, rather than lose a day's pay for a domestic difficulty, some people will take holiday while others will just take the day off. Similarly, some will claim sickness for themselves when really it is their child who is sick.

INTRODUCTION

SOME PROBLEMS WITH MEASUREMENT

- **Difficulties with data appropriateness**
Most absentee statistics are bivariate correlation models when absence is multivariate and complex in nature, yet we assume that the variables are related to each other. For example, we assume that increased stress brings increased absence or that higher sick pay brings about malingering. This may or may not be true but multivariate longitudinal data on absence is difficult and costly to obtain. Sometimes the maths required for proper analysis is beyond the resources of the HR department.

- **Difficulties with assumptions**
There is a danger that you might treat an assumption as a fact or reality. A concept such as *employees can choose whether or not to turn up to work* is still only a concept and not a fact. Similarly, *a strong team culture will reduce absenteeism* is only an assumption and should be treated as such.

THEORIES OF ABSENCE

Like all human behaviour, the causes or determinates of casual absence are exceptionally complex. If a simplistic view is taken, then any strategies introduced are unlikely to achieve their maximum success. Three employees can take a day off on a sunny day in summer, but all for separate reasons. One does not need the money, another needs a break from a stressful job, the third is fulfilling a commitment to take a child to the beach.

If, as a management team, you decide to apply financial pressure to reduce absenteeism you might go some way to encouraging the first employee in our example but you will still have a problem with the remaining two. Here are some theories as to why absence occurs.

- **Economic**
This assumes that people do not like work but need to earn enough to maintain their life style. When they have enough money they will decide not to come to work, because the loss in wages is worth the benefit of a self-awarded casual holiday.

INTRODUCTION

THEORIES OF ABSENCE

- **Equity**

This suggests that employees only put in what they think is fair in all the circumstances. If the employer demands too much, or the conditions are too extreme, the employee will redress the balance by withdrawing labour until his or her *inputs* have been matched.

- **Valence**

In any job there are positives and negatives. If the positives are high then absenteeism will be low and vice versa. For example, high team spirit will have a positive effect on attendance, but low team spirit will lead to increased absenteeism. Similarly, if work is not safe, not challenging or supervisors are uninterested, absence, according to this theory, will increase.

- **Need**

This theory suggests that if employees do not feel essential to the organisation, or valued as individuals, they feel they are not needed at work and consequently can take the odd day off.

THEORIES OF ABSENCE

- **Control**
When employees have very little control over their work, what they do or how they do it, then one way of exercising and taking back control is to withdraw their labour.

- **Work Time Tolerance**
Only so much work and work-associated activity can be tolerated. So work time, overtime and travel to work time combine to a maximum, and when the tolerance level is reached the employee takes time off to recuperate.

- **Life Balance**
Employees work to live rather than live to work, and so they will be keen to preserve a balance in their lives and behave accordingly.

- **Culture**
This suggests that people's levels of attendance are influenced by their social environment and *mores*. Their absences match what is considered to be acceptable or unacceptable in their community, eg: Monday absences are OK, or it is acceptable to view your sick pay entitlement as a right and take the full amount.

THEORIES OF ABSENCE

- **Job Satisfaction**

At a simplistic level this suggests that the more interesting and challenging the job the lower the casual absence. This is thought to be one of the reasons why management absence is less than employee absence.

- **Stress and Safety**

Where jobs are stressful or unsafe absence increases. For instance, this explains why social services (as a staff example) and mining (as a blue-collar example) traditionally have shown higher absenteeism than their colleagues working at a similar level elsewhere.

Thought Point

All the theories are presented in a single factor format, but it is important to appreciate that casual absence by an employee at any one time is an amalgam of a whole host of reasons rather than just a single cause.

A WORD OF CAUTION

With all these absence theories you can see that it is dangerous to favour just one, and thus promote a too-simplistic approach. Any management initiative should take a comprehensive view of the problem, otherwise the intervention will be rather like trying to cover bullet holes with sticky plasters.

If your view is just economic, your solutions will tend towards reducing sick pay entitlement and/or offering attendance bonuses. Conversely, if you have a humanistic perspective, your solutions will be the promotion of job rotation and job enrichment programmes. A management team, as it approaches the problem of absenteeism, can fall victim to the limitations of its own viewpoint.

Action based upon urban myths, personal prejudice, inappropriate axioms and stereotypes is unlikely to have the desired result.

Having examined the theories of absence we now turn to look at absence from the viewpoint of the individual.

NOTES

CAUSES OF ABSENCE

THE INDIVIDUAL

As well as the theories, aspects of the individual also have a bearing. These we now review; but please remember that these are general *all things being equal* suggestions, and are subject to huge variation owing to circumstances both in and outside the workplace.

● **Absence Record**
The best indication of future behaviour is past behaviour, so individuals who have been good attendees usually continue to be so, while the reverse is also true.

● **Age**
Older people tend to be absent less frequently than younger people, but when they are absent the period is of longer duration.

● **Disposition**
There is a suggestion that those who are anxious and emotionally unstable are prone to greater absenteeism. The same is true of those who feel they have little control over their lives.

CAUSES OF ABSENCE

THE INDIVIDUAL

- **Gender**
Early studies suggested that females were absent more than males. Later studies revealed that as females become older, their absence dropped back to similar levels to males, suggesting that absence has more to do with the responsibilities of motherhood and family than just gender.

- **Seniority**
The longer a person stays with an organisation the lower his or her absence level tends to be. This is complicated when there is a service requirement before entitlement to sick pay, but by and large it is valid.

- **Travel to Work Time**
The longer it takes someone to get to work the higher that person's absence rate. Interestingly, the closer someone lives to work the greater his or her tardiness. Also, the more complicated the travel to work in terms of changes, say from bus to train, the higher the absenteeism.

- **Smokers**
Smokers can have as much as 46% higher absence than non-smokers.

(17)

CAUSES OF ABSENCE

THE INDIVIDUAL

- **Personality**
The evidence here is not so definite, but it would appear that extroverts have a higher absence level than introverts and that stable introverts have the lowest absence of all.

- **Personal work ethic**
The Protestant work ethic suggests that individuals are committed to their work, want to do well and their success shows that they have not wasted the talents that God has given them. For such individuals the absence rate is very low – it is almost a sin to take time off work, unless you are very ill or under considerable domestic strain.

- **Personal Wealth**
The more someone is financially independent of their work remuneration, the more cavalier he or she is about casual absence.

Thought Point
Care has to be taken here that a policy or a selection activity that attempts to address these causes does not fall within the bounds of discrimination.

CAUSES OF ABSENCE

THE WORKPLACE

- **Job content**

In manufacturing work particularly, jobs have been reduced to their most simple structures. This has led to alienation of the worker from the end result of his or her labour. Jobs become boring, repetitive, routine, fragmented, requiring minimum ability. In such situations, commitment or loyalty to work or pride in one's labour is minimal, job satisfaction is non-existent and rather than suffer from *rust out* employees seek stimulation outside work. Days off provide relief from the monotony of work.

- **Stress Content**

Where the job is stressful or dangerous, there is a tendency for employees to provide respite for themselves by taking additional time off work, which is the best way of reducing stress and providing a safe environment.

- **Team Cohesion**

As a rule of thumb, the larger the organisation the higher the absence level.
This could occur for two reasons:

1. As the teams get larger there is greater opportunity for anonymity
2. The larger the workforce the more specialised the work

CAUSES OF ABSENCE

THE WORKPLACE

- **Job Change**

Groups provide an opportunity for friendship, group identification and the development of teamworking. Frequent job changes disrupt this opportunity for a group's social integration as well as the possibility of mutual co-operation, and so absenteeism is more likely.

- **Quality of Management**

The role of the first line manager in the control of absence is crucial, so the quality of this level of management has a huge impact on absence. Quality management is required not just for the simple things such as record-keeping, but also for counselling employees who have been absent, challenging when necessary, and being fair and reasonable when following the disciplinary procedure.

- **Job Satisfaction**

This is more a popular belief than a well-documented theory. At face value, the more you dislike or are dissatisfied with your job, the greater the tendency to take time off. The difficulty here is that this proposition is not supported by the research literature.

CATEGORIES OF ABSENCE

Absence is normally thought of as sickness absence but, although there are some people who will abuse their sick pay entitlement, most malingering is in casual absence. To be able to tease out types of absence, company black spots, and aberrant employees, you need to set up systems to identify the type and frequency of absence taken by every employee.

Here are some categories of absence:

Holidays and Sickness
Annual leave
Holiday leave
Extended leave with permission

Certified sick
Self-certified sick
Work accident
Approved appointments: doctor, hospital, dentist, ante-natal, optician, chiropodist, other

Training and development
Day release
Examination leave
Off the job training: in-company, ex-company
Study leave

Continued ▶

CATEGORIES OF ABSENCE

Employee relations
Committee work: consultative, safety
Lay off
Lieu day
Secondary industrial action
Stood down
Short time
Strike: official, unofficial
Suspended: without pay, with pay
Union duties: union member, union
representative

Personal
Bereavement
Compassionate
Maternity
Paternity

Community
Civic duties
Jury service
Military service
Territorial Reserve

Casual
Absence for unknown reason
Unauthorised absence

One wants to attack this last category first.
However, what usually happens as you bring
pressure to bear in this group is that there is a
sudden increase in self-certified illness.
Aberrant employees are just moving
themselves from one set of figures into
another, hoping to be able to continue taking
the odd day off.

CAUSES OF ABSENCE

THE GOLDEN DOZEN

Following these pages, you will find no less than 60 suggestions on things that you can do to reduce absenteeism. To misquote Abraham Lincoln:

Some of the measures will work with some of the people some of the time, but none of them will work with all of the people all of the time

That is the bad news. The good news is there are some golden principles that, if you put them into practice according to your specific situation, should bring you success.

1. Absence must be measured

2. All managers and employees must be treated alike

3. Commitment of line management is essential

4. Individual needs and circumstances must be considered

5. Employees need to be encouraged to attend

THE GOLDEN DOZEN

6. Good attendance requires recognition
7. Employees must work in a safe environment
8. Employee discipline must be fair and reasonable
9. Absence information should be public; individuals need feedback
10. Pay should be related to time spent at work
11. Consistency should be maintained and precedents followed
12. Trade unions and employees should be consulted about any scheme before its introduction

THE METHODS

THE METHODS

INTRODUCTION

Set out in this section are 60 practical suggestions you can follow to help reduce absenteeism.

They are divided into groups as follows:

THE METHODS

MANAGEMENT PRELIMINARIES

Have an absence policy
Set an absence objective
Train your management
Train your supervision
Get union support

1: Have an absence policy

This need not be complex but needs to be stated and communicated to employees, especially when they begin their employment. All you need is a simple and straightforward statement, along the lines of:

'It is the policy of the Company that everyone should fulfil their contractual hours and only be absent from work when they are ill, when they are under significant domestic difficulty or for some other good reason. Casual absence by anyone is not acceptable.'

MANAGEMENT PRELIMINARIES

2: Set a total absence objective of 3.5%

Specific objectives are much better than woolly statements such as 'keeping absence down to a minimum'. They give everyone a standard to work towards.

Of course people are going to be off work – they get sick, have babies, have domestic crises but, as a benchmark, 3.5% is about as good as you can reasonably expect.

MANAGEMENT PRELIMINARIES

3: Train your management in the cost of absenteeism

It is surprising that line managers, while often aware of the costs of poor quality, waste, etc, are frequently ignorant of the costs of absenteeism.

If managers know how much things cost, and are held accountable for that cost then this encourages appropriate management action.

MANAGEMENT PRELIMINARIES

4: Train your supervision and first line management in absence control management

First line management and supervision are the key to absence control. Not only do they need to know the absence policy but also they must own it. They are the ones who will operate the control procedures; they must be confident in doing so. Successful schemes are dependent on recording and counselling systems, which must be carried out efficiently and with empathy.

Employees who take advantage of the system will eventually fall foul of the disciplinary procedure and, worst case scenario, it will be line management and supervision who will have to convince the industrial tribunal that they behaved reasonably and fairly in all the circumstances. This will require training.

THE METHODS

MANAGEMENT PRELIMINARIES

5: Have an absence agreement as part of your work practices with the trade union

Reductions in absence will certainly increase profitability, part of which can be given back to employees in improved remuneration.

Also, as you begin to move into the disciplinary procedure with those who continually take unauthorised absence, the process will be easier if you have an agreement with your trade union. It would be a very rare shop steward who would publicly assist management in a member's dismissal, but informally they can do great work explaining to their members the agreed position.

Shop stewards, as well as first line managers, get badgered by employees who are fed up with those who take advantage of the system and let their colleagues down or, through their absence, create extra work for those who are more honest.

PREPARATORY TRAINING

Counselling training

Disciplinary training

Induction training

6: Train your managers in counselling skills

Most unexpected employee absence is for good reasons rather than *lead-swinging*. First line managers need to be empathetic to the needs of their employees who are going to need help or advice, or both. Employees will prefer to unburden themselves to someone they know and respect. This is more likely to be their manager than someone in HR whom they only see occasionally. Not all managers can become counsellors overnight, but they could and should be the first port of call for an employee whenever possible.

If they are going to confront the absenteeism of their employees, managers need to show genuine concern, since most absence, as we have said, will be genuine. It is unreasonable to expect line management to participate actively in the absence control process unless they have been trained in this essential skill.

PREPARATORY TRAINING

7: Train your managers in the disciplinary aspects of absence

Most managers are confident when applying the disciplinary procedure to misconduct items, such as poor performance or safety issues. However, when it comes to absence they feel less certain. They need to be taken through what they can and cannot do, what is and what is not reasonable, and of course the necessary paperwork.

It must always be remembered that dismissed employees have the absolute right to test management's decision in an industrial tribunal. It saps management's confidence if they lose for procedural reasons, when someone really has been taking advantage of the system.

PREPARATORY TRAINING

8: Include the company attendance policy in the induction training

Make sure that each new employee knows the attendance policy and that casual absence will attract the disciplinary procedure. All new employees, unless they are told, will expect the organisation to have the same attitude towards absence as their last employer.

You need to ensure that the standard you expect is communicated at the start of employment, **not** when the employee starts to take time off because he or she was under the impression that it was acceptable to do so.

PREPARATORY TRAINING

9: During induction, when advising employees of the disciplinary and appeals procedure, draw their attention especially to the absence provision in the misconduct section

Employees, unless they are fresh from school or college, will have worked under the disciplinary procedure of other firms which might not have taken absence so seriously.

By using your policy as an example, you ensure that the full attendance requirement is made known.

SELECTION PROCEDURES

References
Health checks
Interview questions
Local people
Resident people
Appropriately qualified
Appropriate personality
Attendance background
Non-smokers

10: Include a specific absence question on the employee form

The best indicator of future performance is past performance. Taking on a new job does not mean that people change either their values or their work behaviour. The question has to be as specific as possible. For example:

'How many days' absence did this person have last year excluding holidays?'

'How many days' sickness did this person have last year?'

THE METHODS

SELECTION PROCEDURES

11: Introduce a pre-employment health questionnaire and medical

This does not guarantee that you only hire fit people, but it certainly increases the likelihood of doing so. Questions again should be specific to the job, for example:

'Can you lift 20 kilos on a regular basis?'
- for someone who labours

'Have you ever suffered from varicose veins?'
- for someone who stands all day

'Have you ever suffered from skin complaints?'
- for someone working with industrial oils

'Do you suffer from headaches?'
- for someone doing visual inspection

In addition, there should be a statement similar to the following:

Misrepresentation of a prior known or treated condition will lead to dismissal irrespective of length of service.

SELECTION PROCEDURES

12: Ask specific questions about attendance at interview

Of course, no one will admit to a poor attendance record, unless they do not want the job, but asking the question preconditions the prospective employee to understand that attendance is important. Again, specific questions are better than those of a general nature, eg:

'Apart from holidays, how many days did you have off work last year?'

'Have you ever been disciplined for either absence or lateness?'

'What do you think your employment reference is going to say about your work attendance?'

SELECTION PROCEDURES

13: Recruit only those who live near the company

Research and statistics suggest that the more difficult it is to get to work, or the longer it takes, the higher the incidence of absence. This can readily be checked against your own records, providing you match employees appropriately and, if it is true, it is easily built into the hiring procedure.

You can also look at how far away someone is from a bus stop or a train station, or how many changes have to be made to get to work. When it is difficult to get to work, or it is a really foul day, travel inconvenience can just tip the balance in favour of absenteeism.

SELECTION PROCEDURES

14: Recruit only settled employees

Potential employees who have just moved into the area may be desperate for work, just to ensure an income flow while they settle into the new area. If they don't settle they will be disenchanted, the absence level will increase, and they will move on or back to where they came from.

This is really tough on newcomers, many of whom could be great employees with wonderful attendance records, but we are playing the averages here. Unfortunately, those who are new to an area have enough problems settling in. Work is not at the forefront of their priorities.

SELECTION PROCEDURES

15: Do not recruit the over-qualified

One of the major reasons for absenteeism is boredom. If you are bright, but working in a brain-numbing job, the only way you are going to get relief is by taking time off. *Rust out* is as much a cause of stress as *burn out*. Unless there is potential for development, promotion or a career, do not be tempted to take on those with more brainpower than the job requires.

Remember that, by and large, brighter people will present themselves better during selection because they are usually more fluent and will be more 'interview astute'. Line managers are particularly prone to being seduced by a brighter than needed candidate, who later will not only be absent but will move on to another job elsewhere.

THE METHODS

SELECTION PROCEDURES

16: Recruit appropriate personalities

You do not have to be a psychologist to do this. All things being equal, introverts prefer to spend time inside their heads and tend not to need social stimulation, while extroverts enjoy social interaction.

If this is so, then a little thought about the type of work will help you in your hiring decision and the subsequent attendance patterns. A high degree of teamwork would be suitable for the extroverts, whereas, should the work be highly repetitive and individual, introverts would be better able to work on their own.

THE METHODS

SELECTION PROCEDURES

17: Beware certain illnesses

Some illnesses are favourites with malingerers because they are hard to prove, and all doctors must take any medical complaint seriously. Consequently, if anyone says they have back pain, which is easy to say but difficult to prove, then the only thing the doctor can reasonably do is advise taking time off work. Migraines fall into the same category.

It is really unfortunate that casual absentees have made it difficult for those with genuine problems who seek jobs.

The wise selector must 'take a view' based on information from:

- The interview
- References
- Pre-medical questionnaire
- Employment medical

Because the last thing you want to do is to recruit your future absentee problem.

THE METHODS

SELECTION PROCEDURES

18: Recruit only non-smokers

This is pretty tough on smokers but it is not discriminatory. Smoking does not fall into the same category as gender, religion, ethnic origin, etc.

Why do it? Because smokers have significantly more days' absence through illness than non-smokers. The main thrust of this Pocketbook is to reduce casual absence, but why recruit people who, on average, have greater absenteeism?

CONTRACTUAL OPPORTUNITIES

Access to employee's doctor
Absence as misconduct
Disciplinary procedure
Sick pay arrangements
Redundancy selection

19: Include access to employee's doctor in the absence procedure

Part of the employee's terms and conditions of employment should be agreement to the company's absence policy and procedures. This should include a statement to the effect that, should there be extensive absence or regular patterns of absence, the employee will give permission for the company to contact his or her GP.

The usual confidentiality protocol of course applies, as to who has access to the information, how long it is kept, etc.

THE METHODS

CONTRACTUAL OPPORTUNITIES

20: Include unauthorised or casual absence in the misconduct section of the disciplinary procedure

Usually, absence is not thought serious enough to be included in the list of misdemeanours that go into the misconduct category.

Including it achieves two things: first, it hammers home the message that people are expected to fulfil their contractual hours. Second, it makes discipline easier than when you have to attempt to include it under the statement: *this list is not exhaustive but should be taken as an illustration,* which rounds off most misconduct lists.

CONTRACTUAL OPPORTUNITIES

21: Include failure to follow company absence procedures as misconduct in the disciplinary procedure

Dismissal on grounds of capability is far more difficult to justify than dismissal for conduct. Aberrant employees will push the system to the limits but will find the absence reporting and control systems (suggestions 44, 45 and 46) difficult and consequently will avoid them.

By making the procedures mandatory, it provides another way of dealing with this type of employee, avoiding the difficulties surrounding dismissal for employee capability.

CONTRACTUAL OPPORTUNITIES

22: Make sick pay less than normal pay

If an employee is sick then their requirement for their disposable income is reduced. It makes little sense to pay someone the same amount when they are sick as when they are at work. On the other hand it would be somewhat draconian to pay them nothing while they are away sick. Everybody gets sick sometime and you don't want people to drag themselves to work because they cannot afford to be ill.

It is suggested that sick pay needs to be reduced to 30% to 35% of average pay (provided you observe statutory minimum requirements). This allows people to meet their financial obligations in the short-term, but does not make it profitable for them to extend their absence any longer than necessary.

CONTRACTUAL OPPORTUNITIES

23: Have absence as a significant factor which is taken into consideration when it comes to selection for redundancy

Normally, in the absence of any policy, most firms, encouraged by the unions, operate on LIFO – Last In First Out. However, it is perfectly legitimate for firms to set a redundancy selection procedure, providing employees know about it well beforehand.

It would be unfair, in a redundancy situation, for a long-standing employee to be terminated on the grounds of a poor attendance record, if they were told of the arrangement for the first time only when they asked 'Why me?'. Sometimes line managers are under the misapprehension that redundancy somehow is exempt from the unfair dismissal provisions. They have not appreciated that redundancy is in fact a form of dismissal and consequently has to be fair in all the circumstances.

HEALTH MATTERS

Recruit an occupational nurse
Appoint a company doctor
Health reviews
Welfare visits
Health Committee
Request certificates
Health programmes

24: Recruit a qualified nurse into the HR Department

For the larger firm this can be a position in its own right; for the smaller organisation he or she can hold one of the HR positions. With such a qualified person on site good health advice is on tap and readily available.

With stringent absence arrangements there could be a tendency for employees to come to work when they really should be away sick. The nurse's advice here would be invaluable.

HEALTH MATTERS

25: Appoint a company doctor

Look for someone who is interested in occupational health, and give him or her a full induction to all the types of work that are required by the company. Your new doctor will be able to make suggestions as to whether an employee is fit for work or not.

He or she can contact the employee's doctor and explain the nature of the person's work, as well as assist in the health reviews and give advice on the difficult decisions about capability.

(51)

THE METHODS

HEALTH MATTERS

26: Set up a health review system

You cannot discipline people for being sick because everyone is sick sometimes. However, there will be some who are regularly sick; somehow for exactly the maximum of their annual sick pay entitlement. This might be coincidental but needs to be tested. There will also be people whose backache always occurs on a Friday and lasts only one day, or who somehow manage to have a migraine every time their football team has a midweek away game. These people always have 'doctor's papers' to justify their absence.

For such people you need a series of health reviews to see if they are fit enough to do the jobs for which they have been recruited. This is not easy, because to dismiss for capability is difficult. It goes something like the following:

1st health review: Discussion with the nurse about health and sickness patterns.

HEALTH MATTERS

26: Set up a health review system (cont'd)

2nd health review: With permission, your company doctor contacts the employee's doctor to gain a long-term view of the difficulty. Written warning given that if absence patterns continue the employee may not be capable of doing the job on health grounds.

3rd health review: With permission from employee's doctor, contact all parties concerned, saying that if the situation is unlikely to improve in the foreseeable future employee will be released from employment on health grounds.

The time between reviews must be reasonable, and at all times the employee's best interest must be paramount. Line management must also understand that releasing someone on health grounds is still dismissal by another name, and the employee is rightly protected from unfair and arbitrary behaviour.

HEALTH MATTERS

27: Welfare visits to the sick from the nurse or someone from the HR Department

This is double-edged. It is an opportunity to show care and concern for the sick individual, and also acts as a deterrent to those who only pretend to be sick. It is best if the person who visits the absentee is someone who is known by the employee, and takes some small gift or posy at the same time.

Those who are supposed to be ill but are not at home will have to explain not only their absence from work but also their absence from home.

HEALTH MATTERS

28: Set up a health committee which decides on the payment of sick pay and other compassionate remuneration

Fellow employees are likely to be more rigorous than managers in the operation of this duty. It will also ensure parity and equity across the organisation. You can hoodwink management but it is far harder to con your fellow employees.

HEALTH MATTERS

29: Request doctor's certificates

When an employee takes continual odd days off or has a regular Monday absence, after so many occurrences he or she should be asked to provide a medical certificate in addition to self-certification. (Management's right to this should be included in the absence policy and procedure that the employee agrees to on joining the company.)

The job of the doctor is to get his or her patient well, so it is a case of certificates on demand, especially in those difficult illnesses such as backache or headache. It is just as difficult for a doctor to spot a malingerer as it is for a line manager. But it just makes it more inconvenient for the malingerer, every time a day off is taken, to go and see the doctor. It adds to the employee's 'social cost' of absence.

HEALTH MATTERS

30: Hold regular health programmes and 'give up smoking' days

This is unlikely to have a significant effect on absence, but is a good way of endorsing the importance of attendance. It shows how seriously the organisation regards the health of its employees, which the good employer should do anyway.

ABSENCE REPORTING

HR responsibility for statistics
Record reasons for absence
Track absence patterns
Monthly reports
Use colours
Communicate to employees
Publish league table

31: Employment statistics should be maintained by the HR Department

Where individual managers are responsible for maintaining the attendance figures inconsistency is bound to creep in. When one of their members is heading for a disciplinary hearing because of absenteeism the union will claim, probably correctly, that this particular manager has been more rigorous than others in his or her record-keeping.

ABSENCE REPORTING

32: Within the records, keep notes on reasons for permitted absence

Malingerers can afford to have a poor memory, but you can't. This is best explained by a true story. A young woman in a plant where I was HR director informed the occupational health nurse that she wanted Friday off to go to her grandmother's funeral.

This seemed a very reasonable request, but it was challenged with 'Well, which one are you digging up? According to the records you attended the funerals of both your grandmothers last year!!?'.

ABSENCE REPORTING

33: Track absence patterns for employees

Mondays and Fridays are very popular days for casual absence, for obvious reasons. Some people will take a day off a month almost as an entitlement. Others will take the time off when the sun shines or the local football team is playing an away game. Most people are creatures of habit, and when their casual absence habits are challenged (they know that you know), it is usually sufficient to change their behaviour.

By the same token, managers should not be away when there is a local golf championship. Golf days with clients, when half the management is away on a junket, are not likely to encourage employees to improve their attendance behaviour.

Sometimes a regular pattern of absence – and lateness – can be an early sign of an alcohol problem.

THE METHODS

ABSENCE REPORTING

34: Report absence figures to your management on a regular basis, and not less than once per month

Management cannot do anything unless they know. Information is only effective when it leads to action. It is one thing to know about your absence figures but another to do something about it.

Figures should be published on the various reports that are made on a regular basis, in the same way that the figures for production, quality, wastage, accidents, slow moving stock or debt collection days are made known.

If the absence figures are not important enough to be communicated, then the problem will not be thought significant enough to be acted upon.

ABSENCE REPORTING

35: Communicate to your management in colours

Your management and first line supervision are bombarded with numbers all day long in their daily work. Whether absence is at 4.76% or 6.32% is neither here nor there. What you want is for your management to take action; so give them the figures but colour code them, eg:

Absence at 6.6% plus   - Red
Absence at 4.6% to 6.5% - Orange
Absence at 3.0% to 4.5% - Green

ABSENCE REPORTING

36: Communicate to employees each year the amount of pay they have lost, because of absence during the previous year

Taking the odd day here or there might not have much impact on pay, but when it is aggregated over a year the amount can appear significant enough to affect behaviour. Rather like the amount spent on smoking – each day the amount may not be large but over a year it mounts up dramatically.

In the USA this information is sometimes made available to the spouse. This is mentioned out of interest and is not a recommendation!!

ABSENCE REPORTING

37: Publish league table of success

Who are the best individuals or departments? Let them celebrate their success by mentioning them in dispatches. Just as one might have a notice about the department with the most accident-free days, why not publicise attendance success in the same way?

INCENTIVES

Gala Dinner
Attendance bonus
Attendance raffle
Absence bank
Group bonus
Holiday arrangements

38: Have a gala dinner for those with perfect attendance in the year

This shows appreciation in a tangible way. A dinner is better than an outing during the firm's time because this would be *absence* in another form and send out the wrong message. Better still if you can invite spouses and partners, because a year without absence probably could not have been achieved without their support and co-operation.

THE METHODS

INCENTIVES

39: Give a bonus for attendance

This is very popular with some firms, but there is a fair amount of evidence to suggest that its impact on attendance is short-lived. Also, when it no longer works, the trade union, not unexpectedly, negotiates hard for the bonus element to be consolidated into the basic wage.

There are also philosophical and practical questions that need to be thought through, such as:

● Why should you pay for people to do what they are contracted to do in the first place?

● Doesn't this put the initiative on whether or not to attend into the hands of the employee who could take the view that, as he or she chooses not to receive the bonus, he/she is entitled to be absent?

● If someone misses a day through no fault of their own, then their opportunity for earning the bonus has been lost. If their attendance is in the balance on a subsequent day, the fact that they have already lost their bonus just might tip their decision in the wrong direction.

THE METHODS

INCENTIVES

40: Have an attendance raffle

The names of all those who have achieved perfect attendance are put into a hat and a winner is drawn. If the prize is significant enough it will motivate some but not all.

This moves slightly away from the conundrum of rewarding people for what they should be doing in the first place. However, those who have been absent through no fault of their own are denied the opportunity, and thus for these employees the encouragement to attend will be minimal.

INCENTIVES

41: Have a paid absence bank

Where an employee puts in perfect attendance for an agreed extended period of time, this can be converted into additional holidays or cashed within a set time.

Logically, it does not make sense to reward people for not taking time off by giving them additional time off. It is included here because it has been tried with some, but not great, success.

THE METHODS

INCENTIVES

42: Make the attendance bonus for work groups rather than for individuals

For this to have the greatest effect it is important that the group is not too large, and all the members identify one with another or are in some sort of 'psychological relationship'.

The thinking here is that the individual will not wish to let the group or team down and, in cases of deliberate malingering, the team members will exercise peer group pressure on the aberrant employee.

INCENTIVES

43: When two or more employees want the same holiday week, the person with the best attendance record has first choice over the others

Having been at work more, the employee with the better attendance record deserves the break from work.

Taking holidays when you wish to is particularly valued by employees, and so this small measure will greatly assist an attendance initiative.

THE METHODS

MANAGING THE PROCESS

Reporting to line managers
Reporting early
Work cover
Holiday bookings
Necessary appointments

44: Employees must call their line managers themselves, as early as possible on the first day of absence

It is so easy to suffer from '24 second flu'. This is the time it takes for a family member or friend to call a junior in the HR department (whom they do not know from Adam), and tell a lie about the medical condition of the employee.

It is more difficult for the employee to suffer from such maladies if he or she has to report in personally to a known colleague/manager. Anyone can tell a lie to a stranger and not feel any emotional embarrassment; it is far more difficult to be untruthful to someone who knows you.

Also, from the manager's point of view, if you know someone you are more able to gauge the veracity of their condition.

MANAGING THE PROCESS

45: Employees must call in before the beginning of their shift, or within the first hour of its commencement

One of the significant costs of absenteeism is the reallocation of staff. Line management need to know what manpower resources they have as early as possible, so that they can be as effective as possible.

Failure to follow this procedure should be taken very seriously.

MANAGING THE PROCESS

46: Review the arrangements for who does the employee's work while he or she is away

There is a real difference between coming back and being able to make a fresh start, and coming back to a pile of work that has built up while you have been away.

If someone does your work while you're away, it just goes to endorse the idea that your presence is not really that important.

(73)

MANAGING THE PROCESS

47: Holidays must be booked in advance

When they feel like a day off, some employees ring in and say that they will take it as holiday. This has most of the costs associated with absenteeism: people have to be moved round, quality is not as high, etc.

Of course there will be genuine crises for people: sick children, car breakdowns, etc, but these reasons for absence should be treated as reasonable and with empathy, because no one has a charmed life. Holidays are for rest and relaxation and not to cover domestic difficulties.

MANAGING THE PROCESS

47: Holidays must be booked in advance (cont'd)

If you do not have a payment system for your employees similar to that of your management then in times of crisis, when they are forced to take time off, they will have the double whammy of losing a day's pay. It would be natural to ask for holiday pay in this situation. If you want to introduce this recommendation of only allowing holidays which have been booked in advance, some provision has to be made to address the issue of pay. It would be unreasonable to add a financial difficulty to a domestic crisis.

A word of caution: sometimes line management will connive with employees to take last minute holidays because it makes their absence figures look good. You need administrative systems to cover this.

MANAGING THE PROCESS

48: Gain co-operation for necessary appointments

Doctors, dentists, locksmiths, special deliveries are a fact of life and appointments with them take us away from work. However, with a little bit of planning and co-operation they don't need a whole day's absence.

Appointments first or last thing mean that a significant part of the day can still be at work.

Employees are to be encouraged to book and make appointments which minimise hours lost. For hospital and other medical specialists the HR department, or better still the occupational health nurse, can give the employee a letter requesting an appointment that ensures the minimum number of hours are lost.

TRIGGER MECHANISMS

First absence

Overtime

Absence reviews

Double the average

49: Make a big song and dance on the first occasion of suspected casual absence

What usually happens is that the employee is absent three or four times before being challenged. By this time it is usually too late, for the embryo habit has already been formed.

Much better to start as you mean to go on. Some employees will push the boundaries just to see what they can get away with, and then this becomes their standard.

THE METHODS

TRIGGER MECHANISMS

50: Individual overtime rate will only trigger when an employee has completed a full week's working hours

This prevents an employee 'catching up' on wages. For example, if he or she takes Monday off for no good reason, but then on Saturday works four hours at *time and a half,* the amount of money out of pocket is minimal.

With this suggestion, the individual would have to work all day Saturday – the equivalent of a full week – before overtime payment would trigger.

TRIGGER MECHANISMS

51: Have absence reviews

A certain level of absence should trigger an absence review with someone in HR. Similarly, when there have been a set number of absences, irrespective of the duration, over a set period this also should trigger an absence review.

Hopefully the absences will be either justified or permissible, but this will capture those who are taking advantage.

THE METHODS

TRIGGER MECHANISMS

52: Regularly review all employees, individually, who have double the average absenteeism, or absenteeism that is in the third standard deviation away from the norm

Employees soon work out what is an acceptable absenteeism rate because, like sheep in a field, they keep testing the boundaries. Absence will slowly increase until they are challenged. Then they will know what the boundary is – what is acceptable and what is not.

The way around this is to have a moving boundary so that no one can work it out. If you see everyone who is twice the average, or at the third standard deviation and beyond, you will be continually spotlighting the worst employees, who will either improve or fall foul of the disciplinary procedure. Either way attendance improves. As the total absence falls back to 3.5%, there is a danger that it will hover above that figure. This process will go some fair way to keeping the figure dropping.

Congratulate and commiserate
Each year write to congratulate and thank all those who have put in a good year of attendance – say the best 10%. Write to the worst 10% expressing concern about their absence and their health, confirming that they will be monitored in the coming year.

PERFORMANCE & PROMOTION

Performance reviews
Reviews for management
Promotion

53: Make attendance part of all employees' performance review

This complements the effort of letting all the new starts know how important it is to be at work for their contractual hours, since it is more likely to be the established employees who will have a performance review.

Hopefully it will provide the appraising manager with the opportunity of thanking and congratulating the appraisee for an excellent attendance record.

PERFORMANCE & PROMOTION

54: Make personal absence, and absence control, part of management's performance review

What is good for the goose is also good for the gander. Management, especially when they are highly visible to those whose absence you wish to reduce, must also be held to account for their personal performance, as regards both their own absence and the absence of those who report to them.

PERFORMANCE & PROMOTION

55: Do not promote anyone whose attendance is poor

It is not uncommon for line managers, especially in production, to spoil their best workers because they produce more. This leniency extends to turning a blind eye to the odd day off.

When it comes to promotion, opportunities naturally fall to the best operators, but if their work was averaged out over the period that they should have been at work, their production figures would not look so encouraging.

MAKE IT EASY

Help employees
Flexitime
Interesting jobs
Teamworking
Increase skills

56: Assist employees to meet their family obligations

It may be possible to change the shift arrangements to coincide with school hours or school holidays. Perhaps you could have a 'bank' of two days when employees could take time off for reasonable domestic crises. Not that this would reduce absenteeism because some would abuse it, but for the majority it would create a culture of care and concern.

This would certainly go a long way to making employees feel that they did not have to lie to get time off.

THE METHODS

MAKE IT EASY

57: Introduce flexible time working arrangements

This can be provided in a variety of ways:

Job sharing – either mornings and afternoons, or first and last part of the week. This arrangement allows plenty of time outside work to meet all domestic demands and the problems that occur from time to time.

Flexitime – built around a core time, employees can start and finish when they wish as well as having flexibility around their lunch times. Like job sharing, it provides time for all those personal contingencies.

THE METHODS

MAKE IT EASY

58: Make the job more interesting

As we have mentioned before, when
employees are bored they will seek relief
through absence. Where a job can be
expanded, or individuals can be given
more responsibility or the opportunity to
develop more skill, absence will fall.

Consider reducing supervision, allowing
employees to set their own production targets
and/or take responsibility for quality. These are all
ways in which the job can be enriched.

THE METHODS

MAKE IT EASY

59: Introduce teamworking

Putting people into teams develops a sense of obligation to fellow team members and a desire not to let them down. It also means that if the team can be autonomous, that is, making as many decisions for itself as possible, the work becomes intrinsically more interesting. Absence reduces accordingly.

Research suggests that when these measures are introduced the effects on reducing absenteeism are very significant indeed.

MAKE IT EASY

60: Wherever possible, increase your employees' skills

This makes work both challenging, exciting and interesting so it is little wonder that wherever this approach has been tried absence has dropped considerably.

THE METHODS

SUMMARY

WHAT WORKS BEST?

Intervention	% effectiveness
Formal notification procedure	82%
Return to work interviews	73%
Teamworking	70%
Disciplinary procedures	69%
Absence statistics for managers	69%
Not recruiting poor attenders	60%
Occupational health services	58%
Pre-recruitment medicals	56%
Health promotion	42%
Waiting days before sick pay is given	35%
Attendance bonus	34%
Absence as selection for redundancy	28%

NOTES

THE LEGAL BITS

THE LEGAL BITS

BASIC RIGHTS

Under the Employment Rights Act (ERA), as a general rule, employees with more than one year's service hold their jobs as a basic right and cannot be fired arbitrarily. Employers have to show that:

- Dismissal for absence was fair, and
- They acted reasonably in all the circumstances

When it comes to absence, what is meant by *fair* has two categories:

1. **Capability:** is the employee capable of doing the work for which he or she was employed?
2. **Conduct:** is the employee's behaviour such that he or she rejects the contract of employment?

In both situations the employers have to demonstrate that they acted reasonably.

THE LEGAL BITS

DISMISSAL FOR CAPABILITY: ISSUES

This is usually in connection with long-term illness and can be quite complicated. The Tribunal needs to ensure that the employee has been given due care and consideration, and has not lost his or her job through falling ill, which could happen to anyone. A good parallel is to think that an employee owns a job in the same way as he or she might own a house. A job cannot be taken away arbitrarily.

Here are just some of the things that must be reviewed:

- **Length of service:** the longer the service the more compassionate the employer is expected to be.

- **Contract of employment:** especially the provisions for sick pay.

- **Duration of employment:** how long would the work have lasted – would it be less than the anticipated duration of the illness?

- **The type of illness:** what is the nature of the illness or injury?

- **Recovery expectation:** was there definite medical evidence that the illness was going to last an extended period of time and/or that when recovery came the employee would be strong enough to do the job on return?

Continued ▶ (93)

THE LEGAL BITS

DISMISSAL FOR CAPABILITY: ISSUES

- **Employer's situation:** is there another employee who could do the work of the sick person; if so the employer is expected to be more patient. If the work is critical and the employee is unique in the firm, then a more prompt dismissal can be effected.

- **Other positions:** could the employer provide another position which would suit the condition of the employee and would be acceptable to him or her?

- **Remuneration:** has the employer shown by continual payment that there is a desire for the contract of employment to continue.

- **Reasonableness:** in all the circumstances, was the action taken what a reasonable employer would do?

- **Disability:** where an employee has become incapable of doing the job, it may have to be treated as disability.

- **Formal dismissal:** has the employee been taken through a fair and reasonable process in the way that they have been dismissed.

It is the dismissal process that we must now consider.

THE LEGAL BITS

DISMISSAL FOR CAPABILITY: PROCESS

This is a difficult process to handle procedurally. It also needs to be done with genuine concern. Here is a possible outline but, should you decide to dismiss a sick employee, it will be best to take professional advice.

First Health Review

Discuss with employee: nature of illness, possible long-term prognosis, possible work implications. Agree that if the illness/condition is going to continue you may need to consult their doctor. The request to contact the doctor should be made in writing.

Note that the employee:
- Can refuse to give consent.
- Can see the report before it is passed to the employer
- Having seen the report can refuse to let it be seen by the employer
- Can ask for amendments to be made/can attach own comments to the report

Within the company, explore: alternative work opportunities, whether others can do the work of the sick employee, how critical the employee's work is and, given the employee's length of service, how long the company might wait, given the worst case scenario.

THE LEGAL BITS

DISMISSAL FOR CAPABILITY: PROCESS

Second Health Review

Having given permission, the employee should be seen by the company doctor, who should then confer with the employee's own doctor as to the illness and the long-term prognosis.

Note: The employee has the right to refuse to be seen by the company doctor. If this happens, she must be told in writing that a decision will be taken on the information available and that this decision could include dismissal.

The employee's views and concerns about her condition and the implications for her job, are to be sought and actively considered by management. It is important that she is very much part of the process and, where possible, any decision that is made.

Where possible and appropriate, the employee is to be told in writing after the second review that, having considered all the information to hand, should the illness continue, it may be necessary for her employment to be terminated, or that if she will not return to work fit enough to do the job for which she was employed, what other arrangements might be possible.

Important: This is not misconduct and a health review is not a disciplinary discussion. Throughout, concern for the health of the employee should be paramount.

THE LEGAL BITS

DISMISSAL FOR CAPABILITY: PROCESS

Third Health Review

Should there be no improvement in the employee's condition, and/or both doctors agree that the condition will be prolonged or will worsen in the foreseeable future, and the employee agrees with this prognosis, the company can consider dismissal as a last resort. The possibility of keeping the position open permanently, and that of alternative employment, should already have been examined.

At this point, with regret, you must inform the employee that her employment will be terminated with a full notice period. Should there be a significant improvement during the notice period the whole situation will be reviewed.

The employee should be given the right to appeal against this decision, and told how to appeal and what the process will be.

DISMISSAL FOR CONDUCT

Dismissal for conduct is usually for unauthorised absence. Ideally the procedures that are introduced should turn the malingerer into a good employee but, if this is not possible, then the system should be such as to help them malinger elsewhere!

There are two types of casual absence to be dealt with here:

1. Frequent absence with or without certificates

2. Long leaves of absence without permission

DISMISSAL FOR CONDUCT

Frequent absence with or without certificates

Employees should come to work when they are contracted to do so. There is an urban myth that if you have 'doctor's papers' you are bulletproof. Both management and employees need to know that if work is being affected by frequent absence such behaviour can lead to dismissal.

Management must proceed, of course, with both care and fairness, and take into account all the circumstances of the individual case.

The way to proceed would be as follows:

Hold a preliminary review:

- Invite the employee to explain his frequent absences

- Investigate fully any matters arising

- After full consideration, if malingering is suspected, remind the employee of the company's absence policy and procedures and what is expected of the employee

THE LEGAL BITS

DISMISSAL FOR CONDUCT

First review

- If there is no improvement over a reasonable period of time the employee's attendance record is to be reviewed and his explanation requested, investigated and considered.

- If malingering is suspected then the employee is to be told, and informed in writing, that unless his attendance improves, it could lead to a second warning.

- The employee is to be told how to appeal if he feels unfairly treated, that there was no opportunity to state his case or that management have not followed appropriate procedure. If the appeal fails, the employee is to be told in writing why it failed, what the next stage will be and told what is expected of him, as well as the time period over which assessment will take place.

DISMISSAL FOR CONDUCT

Second Review

- If there is no improvement over a reasonable period of time the employee's attendance record is to be reviewed and his explanation reviewed, investigated and considered.

- It may be appropriate to refer the employee to the company doctor (see pages 45, 51, 95 for notes on this).

- If malingering is suspected then the employee is to be told, and informed in writing, that unless his attendance improves it could lead to a final warning.

- The employee is to be told how to appeal if he feels unfairly treated, that there was no opportunity to state his case or that management have not followed appropriate procedure. If the appeal fails, the employee is to be told in writing why it failed, what the next stage will be and told what is expected of him, as well as the time period over which assessment will take place.

DISMISSAL FOR CONDUCT

Third Review

● This should be the same as the second review and unless there is good reason then it will be a final warning

Final Review

● Again the same procedure, but with dismissal with notice

This might seem like a long drawn out procedure but the whole emphasis is on helping the employee to improve rather than trying to dismiss him or her. In my experience, sensible malingerers, if that is not an oxymoron, leave of their own accord. They take this option because they recognise that they are not going to get away with it any longer. They think it will be easier just to get another job, where they can indulge their absence habit without the tag of dismissal for poor attendance.

DISMISSAL FOR CONDUCT
DISCIPLINARY CODE OF CONDUCT

For this procedure to be effective there need to be statements in the misconduct section of the company's disciplinary code of conduct such as:

Persistent absence or lateness with or without medical certificates

The review procedure needs to be in writing and also communicated to employees during induction. Employees should sign that they have been instructed, understand the procedure, and agree to the attendance policy of the company. For example, it would be wise to have the following points included in the absence policy:

The right to refer an employee to a doctor nominated by the company

Should the employee be suspended then this will be on full pay while the enquiries are being made

Any dismissal for this type of absence is to enjoy notice

Managers and supervisors should also be instructed in the procedures and abide by them. Tribunals rightly take a poor view when a firm has a procedure which is then flouted or ignored by management.

DISMISSAL FOR CONDUCT

LONG LEAVES OF ABSENCE WITHOUT PERMISSION

If an employee cannot make work he has a duty to advise the employer and to keep him/her informed of the situation. Consequently, when an employee does not do this it can be deemed that the contract of employment has been frustrated.

However, the employer must make every reasonable effort to contact the employee to discover the circumstances. It would be wise to write and/or visit the employee to see what the situation is and to communicate the implications of the continued absence, which could mean dismissal for the employee. Attempts at contact could also be made through enquiries of work colleagues.

Note: It would also be helpful to have a statement in the absence procedure to the effect: *Where an employee absents him/herself from work for a period beyond 5 working days without informing the company as to the reason for absence the employee will be dismissed.*

THE LEGAL BITS

DISMISSAL FOR CONDUCT

Absence after absence

Some firms provide the opportunity for their employees to take extended leave. Some will take advantage of this by staying away longer than the agreed period.

It is possible for an employee to be dismissed if he or she fails to return to work after a permitted period of extended leave.

The wise employer will have:

- A policy to explain the employment service required to qualify for such leave
- A requirement for a written request for such leave, which also states that the employee understands and agrees to both the policy and the procedure
- A definite limit to the amount of time that can be taken
- A signed statement by the employee that he understands that if he does not return to work on the agreed day for any reason whatsoever his employment will be terminated

Even with the above, it would also be advisable to ensure through a face to face discussion, with an interpreter if necessary, that the employee has had the policy and procedure explained and knows what will happen if there is a failure to return.

NOTES

INTRODUCING ABSENCE CONTROL

THE MAP DIP APPROACH

The **MAP DIP** approach is an acronym that stands for:

M easure
A ssess
P rioritise

D evelop
I ntroduce
P rogress

THE MAP DIP APPROACH

MEASURE

As has been said before, **measurement is the key**. Without it you have no idea of what is happening where, nor will you know whether your actions are having any effect.

With measurement you would know the following:

- Average number of days lost per year
- Average number of absences per year
- Average length of absence
- Department with the worst absenteeism
- Employees with the worst attendance
- Employees with the best attendance
- Whether directs or indirects have the greater absence
- Whether employees, staff or management have the greater absence
- Whether those working in teams or those working alone have the greater absence
- Whether women have greater absence than men or vice versa
- Whether absenteeism increases with job tenure
- Whether there are patterns to absence – certain seasons, certain days, certain occasions

 Continued

 (109)

INTRODUCING ABSENCE CONTROL

THE MAP DIP APPROACH
MEASURE

- Whether some people take exactly their maximum sick pay entitlement every year
- If young employees are away more frequently than older employees
- If older employees are more likely to take extended periods of absence
- Whether attendance improves after a disciplinary warning
- If there is a relationship between strike activity and other absence
- Whether absence 'moves' from casual to self-certified when initiatives are applied
- Whether casual absence increases after a pay rise
- If there is a relationship between a local event (home game) and absence

Measurement will also give you triggers such as:

- The first absence
- The third absence
- The worst 10% of absentee employees
- When to transfer a sick person to the suspense register
- When to review a series of short sickness absences

THE MAP DIP APPROACH

ASSESS

Having measured the size of the problem you can decide what to do about it. There is always a cost to management action, and in the case of absence the benefits have to outweigh the costs. The further your absence figure is from a total of 3%, the more benefit there is to be gained.

Once you have done the measurement, you should also be in a better position to select which strategies to try to give you the result that you require.

Additionally you need to know where the problem is, and so comparisons are needed. Is the problem to do with:

- A particular area such as production, stores, transport, etc
- A particular type of employment such as shift, day work or temporary
- A particular type of employee such as male/female, old/young, senior/junior

It could also be useful to get some comparative data from companies similar to yours and any industry standards, should they be available. This information helps you decide on the policy, procedure and the interventions that you might want to make.

THE MAP DIP APPROACH

ASSESS

Now you know where the main problems are, it is worth spending some time working out the reasons for the absence. Could the absence be to do with:

Job	too stressful, too dangerous, too tiring, the shift pattern, too boring, etc
Employees	too clever, too extrovert/introvert, too old, too young, too well paid, too much sick pay, travel to work too long/complex, etc
Management	no policy, laissez-faire systems, poor record-keeping, poor supervision, weak supervision, supervision 'off site', unco-operative unions
Culture	traditions of high absenteeism, full sick pay entitlement a right, uninterested supervision, management are poor role models, etc
Organisation	minimum team structure, no work norms, no individual responsibility for work, others do work of absentees
Patterns	Monday and Friday absence, full sick pay entitlement, excessive 'fine day' casual absence

Rather than reinvent the wheel, see what other companies with similar problems to yours have done and learn from their experience. If they were to start again, what would they do differently?

THE MAP DIP APPROACH

PRIORITISE

Decide which area or unit you are going to work on first, devise a policy and your procedures, and learn from your mistakes before you move on and introduce the system company-wide.

When attempting to change human behaviour and employee work culture, it is always best to move forward gently, irrespective of whether you have union support or not. Company culture is very similar to most physical objects; if you squeeze they will resist, if you bend them there will be a tendency for them to revert back to their original shapes. Organisational culture is very similar; when it is pushed or bent there is a tendency for it to revert back.

To have an attendance orientated company will take both patience and time.

INTRODUCING ABSENCE CONTROL

THE MAP DIP APPROACH

DEVELOP

Develop the policy and system that you are going to introduce. Put your draft ideas through the consultative committees and/or negotiate with your trade unions.

You will be amazed at how knowledgeable and how constructive your people will be. They know the problems and they also probably know who, how and why people abuse the system.

What mixture of the following are you going to have?

Positive reinforcement   bonuses, awards, commendation, dinners, prizes, a thank you, etc

Negative reinforcement   challenges, discipline, and loss of perks

Organisational support   recruitment and reference systems, job enrichment, training, multi-skilling, multi-tasking

THE MAP DIP APPROACH

INTRODUCE

Here, you think through the best way to get the scheme off the ground, and implemented into the organisation.

Useful questions might be:

- How is the programme to be introduced?
- How is the programme to be communicated?
- Where is the programme to be introduced?
- Who is going to implement it?
- What training is required and when should it be given?
- What technology back up is required and when will it be available?

115

INTRODUCING ABSENCE CONTROL

THE MAP DIP APPROACH

PROGRESS

Management is like anything else in life: you get things right by getting them wrong. Changing a company culture that has taken years to develop will not be easy and there will be false starts. The programme will have to have both the flexibility and the rigour to be able to reinvent itself, so that it addresses the real problems effectively as they emerge.

Possible questions here would be:

- Where is the programme succeeding and why?
- Are employees and supervision co-operating with both policy and procedures?
- Is there an increase in disciplinary appeals or claims for unfair dismissal because of the procedure?
- Is there a genuine reduction in total absence rather than just an increase in certified sickness and a reduction in casual absence, or an increase in strike activity so that there is no change in the overall figure?
- At what speed is absence being reduced?
- How is the programme affecting morale?
- How is the programme affecting trade union relations?
- Are productivity and quality improving?

HEALTH & SAFETY

Accidents at work contribute significantly to absence both when there is an accident and also when employees feel stressed because they are working in an unsafe environment.

Accidents at work usually occur when employees:

- Do not use safety or protective equipment or clothing
- Use equipment that they know to be unsafe
- 'Push' their equipment beyond the safety limits
- Use the wrong tools for the job, or use their hands inappropriately
- Remove safety shields and sabotage protective systems
- Move or work in incorrect body positions
- Attempt to lift too much
- Undertake what they are not trained to do
- Fail to report near accidents so that precautions and safety systems are not put in place
- Distract workmates from concentrating on their jobs

STATISTICS

- For every £5 an employee loses through absence the employer loses £10

- If your absenteeism is above 4% then it is highly likely that some of your employees are taking advantage of whatever systems you have

- Blue-collar employees on average enjoy an extra week of holiday a year through casual absence

- £20 billion is the estimated cost of absence in Britain per year

- Absence in Britain is significantly higher than in other European countries

JUST THINK

You only have to get one person to come to work on one day when they might have chosen to stay away for this book to make you a handsome return on your small investment.

About the Author

Max A. Eggert
Max is an international management psychologist who specialises in assisting organisations and individuals to achieve their best. He works mainly in the UK and Australia. A respected authority on the human and organisational aspects of change and empowerment, Max has delivered workshops and seminars to thousands of executives and managers throughout the world.

Other books by Max include:
The Managing Your Appraisal Pocketbook; The Assertiveness Pocketbook; The Motivation Pocketbook; The Management and Delivery of Outplacement; The Perfect CV (in top 10 business books); The Perfect Interview; The Perfect Career; The Perfect Consultant; Career Questions; The Australian Résumé.

Contact

Max can be contacted at:
Transcareer Pty Ltd, PO Box 36, Waverley, NSW, 2024 Australia.
Tel: +61 2 9821 1105   Fax +61 2 9821 1106   Mobile: +61 403 602 286
E-mail: max@transcareer.com.au

Other titles by Max Eggert in the Pocketbook series
(see opposite for full listing)

THE MANAGEMENT POCKETBOOK SERIES

Pocketbooks

Appraisals
Assertiveness
Balance Sheet
Business Planning
Business Presenter's
Business Writing
Career Transition
Challengers
Coaching
Communicator's
Controlling Absenteeism
Creative Manager's
C.R.M.
Cross-cultural Business
Cultural Gaffes
Customer Service
Decision-making
Developing People
Discipline
Diversity
E-commerce
E-customer Care

Emotional Intelligence
Employment Law
Empowerment
Energy and Well-being
Facilitator's
Handling Complaints
Icebreakers
Improving Efficiency
Improving Profitability
Induction
Influencing
International Trade
Interviewer's
I.T. Trainer's
Key Account Manager's
Leadership
Learner's
Manager's
Managing Budgets
Managing Cashflow
Managing Change
Managing Upwards

Managing Your Appraisal
Marketing
Meetings
Mentoring
Motivation
Negotiator's
Networking
People Manager's
Performance Management
Personal Success
Project Management
Problem Behaviour
Problem Solving
Quality
Resolving Conflict
Sales Excellence
Salesperson's
Self-managed Development
Starting In Management
Stress
Succeeding at Interviews
Teamworking

Telephone Skills
Telesales
Thinker's
Time Management
Trainer Standards
Trainer's

Pocketsquares

Great Training Robbery
Hook Your Audience
Leadership: Sharing The Passion

Pocketfiles

Trainer's Blue Pocketfile of
Ready-to-use Exercises

Trainer's Green Pocketfile of
Ready-to-use Exercises

Trainer's Red Pocketfile of
Ready-to-use Exercises

ORDER FORM

Your details

Name _____

Position _____

Company _____

Address _____

_____

_____

Telephone _____

Fax _____

E-mail _____

VAT No. (EC companies) _____

Your Order Ref _____

Please send me:

		No. copies
The Controlling Absenteeism	Pocketbook	
The _____	Pocketbook	
The _____	Pocketbook	
The _____	Pocketbook	
The _____	Pocketbook	

Order by Post

MANAGEMENT POCKETBOOKS LTD

LAUREL HOUSE, STATION APPROACH, ALRESFORD,
HAMPSHIRE SO24 9JH UK

Order by Phone, Fax or Internet

Telephone: +44 (0)1962 735573
Facsimile: +44 (0)1962 733637
E-mail: sales@pocketbook.co.uk
Web: www.pocketbook.co.uk

Customers in USA should contact:
Stylus Publishing, LLC, 22883 Quicksilver Drive,
Sterling, VA 20166-2012
Telephone: 703 661 1581 or 800 232 0223
Facsimile: 703 661 1501 E-mail: styluspub@aol.com